INVEST

IN

YOURSELF

INVEST
IN
YOURSELF

Francis A. Tella

XULON PRESS

Xulon Press
2301 Lucien Way #415
Maitland, FL 32751
407.339.4217
www.xulonpress.com

Printed in the United States of America.

ISBN-13: 9781545610954

To God, who called me before I was born.
To Bunor, my wife and love, who has helped me to grow.
To my children, who think I'm the best in the world.
To everyone who has invested in me.

CONTENTS

FOREWORD

AS THE AUTHOR OF THIS BOOK MENTIONS IN THE INTRODUCTION, this masterpiece is an investment in every reader.

I have had the honor of knowing Pastor Francis Akin Tella for quite a few years, and he has been consistent through those years. He is authentic and loyal, and he is one person who is sure to tell you as it is if you are looking to hear the truth. Pastor Akin Tella is also a great man of God who strives for excellence. He is a family man and a pastor with a shepherd's heart. He is sold out to God and takes his calling very seriously.

Pastor Tella was able to write this book, *Invest in Yourself*, as a result of many years in which God and others have invested in him, so you can rest assured that it is filled with a wealth of lessons that God has taken him through. Who can better teach authentically than a man who tells it as it is, without watering down God's word or his personal experiences?

Pastor Akin explains in depth in this book why you should invest in yourself; the right kind of investment to make (every investment is not positive); the importance of your relationship with God (this will affect the outcome of everything else in your life); and the importance of practicing godliness (spiritual training and being attuned to who you are in Christ), investing in your character, and investing in your relationship with others.

He also stresses that you are priceless and worth God's best as he takes you through personalizing God's love for you.

Do yourself a favor by investing in yourself as you read this book, which will help you on your way to becoming all God has called you to be. Don't stop there; invest in someone else, too, by getting them a copy.

I pray that God Himself will minister to you as you read this book inspired by His love.

Pastor Bayo Adewole
Senior Pastor, Jesus House Chicago

INTRODUCTION

THERE IS A PERIOD OF MY EARLY LIFE THAT I TEND TO REFER TO AS the dark ages, and it was almost literally so. It was a period of immense challenge and pain, the memory of which I still sometimes find myself unwittingly struggling to suppress. In order to fully appreciate why this is so, I may have to tell a story of my life, but that is not the intent of this book. There were a number of events that occurred to bring an end to this dark period of my life. One such event was when someone took time to invest in me.

For a number of years while growing up, my family was separated across two continents for what was perceived then as a good purpose. My parents were studying in the United States while my two older sisters, younger brother, and I were scattered and living with family friends in Nigeria. It was a situation that unfortunately created a myriad of challenges for us children, and made us victims of abuse, neglect, and severe maltreatment.

At a point during this time, I was blessed to be staying with the family of a minister friend of my parents in Offa, a city in central Nigeria. I say I was blessed because my eldest sister, Toyin, was also staying with the same family at that time. For me, life was a blur, and painful. I had no understanding of who I was and why I had to go through all the pain, rejection, and maltreatment. Bullied at the home and in school, there was seemingly no escape until my sister started to not only defend and stand for me, but began to tell me again and again what I needed to know about myself. She told me I could stand up for myself anywhere and anytime. She told me I was not a victim or someone to be trampled on by anybody. She invested in me until I understood, believed, and began to stand up for myself. I am eternally grateful that she invested in me.

This book is an investment in you. It is an investment in who you were made to be and in your ability to rise up and become that person. I hope it challenges and motivates you to believe, invest in yourself, and become all you have the potential to be in Christ Jesus.

Chapter 1

WHY SHOULD YOU INVEST IN YOURSELF?

You Are Worth It

YOU ARE INVALUABLE AND DESERVE THE BEST IN LIFE. GOD'S words and actions declare it. If the Creator of the universe considers you worthy of His best, then you must be.

The worth of a thing is typically determined by its value relative to something else. For instance, the value or worth of a currency can be determined by its value when compared to gold or the American dollar. The Bible declares that I am priceless to God. His investment in me is a measure of my worth to Him. First Peter 1:18–20 says to conduct yourselves

> knowing that you were not redeemed with corruptible things, *like* silver or gold, from your aimless conduct *received* by tradition from your fathers, but with the precious blood of Christ, as of a lamb without blemish and without spot. He indeed was

1

foreordained before the foundation of the world,
but was manifest in these last times for you.

You are priceless and worth God's best.

One of the hallmarks of growing up in a conservative Christian environment is the inculcation of a sense of humility born from the belief that we don't deserve anything that we have from God. It is implied that being saved by grace means you deserve nothing and, therefore, are not worth the mercies you have received from God.

In a sense, this is true. However, grace means God considers you worthy of His love and mercies. Therefore, to better appreciate what God has done, it's necessary to see yourself a little differently and realize that regardless of your past, you are worthy of receiving the best that God has for you.

One of my favorite scriptures is John 3:16 "For God so loved the world that He gave His only begotten Son." If you replace "the world" with your name, it becomes more personal. For God so loved me that He gave His best for me! That means in God's eyes, I am worth it. I am worthy of receiving His best. God invested His love in me. Isn't that awesome?

To invest in yourself, you must first believe that you're worth it. God thinks you are, and I agree!

It Will Open the Right Doors for You

Doors symbolize control and access to a place or thing. In some situations, they symbolize authority and dominion, and anyone who controls the door invariably determines who goes in and what they can do. A person who desires access to an exclusive or privileged position would likely need a mentor or sponsor who could assist him or her with the necessary preparation and open some important doors of opportunity. How many times and how often have you wished a certain door was open to you?

Investing in yourself will prepare you to take advantage of the opportunities that God's grace will make come your way.

It Will Help You Live a Successful and Impactful Life

Your life becomes impactful when, through growth, grace, and your own life-molding experiences, you are able to share with others and help them attain more than they could have by themselves. I am convinced that God desires that everyone who walks with Him should be successful and impactful in life. Why? Because it reveals the nature and character of God.

When I grow through my experiences by taking deliberate and ordered steps, I am investing in my life and in God's purpose. Every time you do this, you are adding value to your life, and preparing for a successful future. A person who refuses to grow becomes stagnant and atrophies. The Bible says that we are able to comfort those in trouble when we have received comfort from God ourselves (2 Corinthians 2:14).

It Will Give Perspective and Clarity

Your decisions are impaired and fraught with hazards when you cannot see clearly before making them. Not investing in yourself will make you considerably vulnerable to making regrettable and fatuous decisions at the most crucial moments of life. On the other hand, if you do what is needed to invest in yourself, it will give you a sure footing, enable you to hone your decision-making skills, and provide you with a perspective that enhances right thinking.

The Bible has an interesting story of a man called Nabal.[1] He was married to Abigail, who later became the wife of King David after Nabal died. A subtle comment made by Abigail revealed how bereft of wisdom he was. She said; "For as his name is, so is he: Nabal is his name, and folly is with him." Nabal means foolish.

Nabal's foolishness and petulance was known to all around him, yet he was rich and apparently successful. This trait took on a potentially fatal dimension for him and his family when he spurned David's men and refused to do what was customary for those who helped to protect his livestock. It took a quick-witted servant, a smart Abigail, and the mercies of God to avert what would have been a great disaster and caused the loss of many lives.

Though Nabal was very rich, it did not translate into his dealings with others, because he did not value investing in relationships. When you don't value investing in others, you really cease to invest in yourself. The result is a dangerous self-adulation and lack of perspective that tends to end badly.

It Will Keep You Strong, Stable, and Grounded in an Unstable World

Many dreams and destinies go unrealized because of instability and lack of focus. These are qualities many take for granted, but success in life is almost impossible without them.

I've met many young men and women with great ideas and drive who were lacking in the necessary innate qualities that would have kept them running when the tides of life turned against them. Jesus Christ taught that success in life is not determined by how fast your building goes up or how great it looks. Enduring success comes from a strong and properly built foundation (Luke 6:46–48). This is what ensures that you're still standing when others have been shipwrecked or have caved in to the pressures and distractions of life. Proper investment in yourself is an unequivocal requirement for success in every area of life.

The temptations and challenges of our modern world are continuously evolving and unfurling in diversity and intensity. Only the well-grounded stand any chance of sustained victory. You can be one of this special class of people if you will take the steps needed now and invest in your future.

The Result Speaks for Itself

I occasionally would boast among friends that I understand the Igbo language well. Igbo is the predominant language spoken by people from the eastern part of Nigeria. My wife is of Igbo heritage. The reality, though, is that though I understand the language

5

somewhat, I cannot hold a conversation in it. There are, however, a few words that I know very well. Some of them have taken on a special coded meaning for me and my wife. One of such words is *efulefu*. We use this to describe a person who (or thing that) is without substance and empty—a shell with the appearance of worth, but without real value. That's what a person who hasn't taken the time to build themselves up is like.

The results of quality investments in yourself and your future will be evident to all in good time. Change is evident. Quality speaks. It's the difference between the flame that burns quickly and brightly for a brief moment, and the fire that is sustained and continues to burn and brighten the dark clouds despite the storms. The quality of character is revealed in the dark of the night.

The desire for progress is an intrinsic preoccupation and pursuit of every living being. When a mother gives birth to a child, she wants the baby to grow. The mother watches for every sign of growth and encourages it from the first words, to the first steps, and so on. No sane mother would want a child who has started to talk and walk to regress to the point of not being able to do either. A good investment will grow and show positive results. When this happens, there will be no desire to go back.

It Helps You Attain Your Life's Purpose

I believe that discovering your life's purpose is key to achieving success and significance in life. When you discover the why of your existence, every action, thought, and idea is weighed on the scale of purpose. Otherwise, worthwhile pursuits become meaningless—and a waste of precious resources—because there is something more valuable that you should be doing now.

God, who created you, desires that you will be successful in life and fulfill the purpose for which you were created. Investing in yourself the right way will enable you to be well-rounded, prepared, and furnished with the right qualities that will enable the discovery and fulfilment of your God-given purpose. God wants His children to "be complete and proficient, outfitted and thoroughly equipped for every good work" (2 Timothy 3:17, AMP).

God Has Provided So Much for You to Take Advantage Of

One more reason why you should, by all means, invest greatly in yourself is because of what God has already done for you. Through His love and wisdom, God has already provided for everything that those who belong to Him will need for every stage of life. In fact, the Bible says in 2 Peter 2:2 that the Lord Jesus has "given to us all things that *pertain* to life and godliness, through the knowledge of Him who called us by glory and virtue."

Since the provision is already made, how do I access what I need? How can I maximize the opportunities that the Lord has provided? How can I attain unto all that is possible for me in Christ? The answers lie in making the proper investments and following through with what each demands.

Are you ready?

Notes

1 Samuel 25:2–38

Chapter 2

THE RIGHT INVESTMENTS TO MAKE

Do not lay up for yourselves treasures on earth, where moth and rust destroy and where thieves break in and steal; but lay up for yourselves treasures in heaven, where neither moth nor rust destroys and where thieves do not break in and steal. For where your treasure is, there your heart will be also. (Matthew 6:19–21)

The Value of the Right Kind of Investment

A GOOD INVESTMENT BANKER FIRST SEEKS TO UNDERSTAND THE objective of his prospective client before offering advice on what might be the right mix of investments to make. A potential investor will be well advised to run from an adviser who does not first take time to understand the investor's objectives and risk tolerance. Why is this important? Your objectives determine what kind of investment will be the right fit for you. What are your objectives for reading this book, going to school, or doing what you are currently engaged in?

Many years ago, while talking with our sons about their goals and objectives, as every parent tends to do, we asked our younger son Joshua the age-old question: what do you want to be when you grow up? His response was simple. "I want to be famous," he said with a look of serious contemplation on his face. It caught us by surprise, and we couldn't contain ourselves; we laughed before proceeding to explain that being famous is not an appropriate goal in the context of our discussion.

I hope your objective is not achieving fame or notoriety. I hope it is a more substantive, tangible, and credible goal. If it is, then this is the right book for you. Better yet, I will suggest making the following your goal: *that Christ will be magnified in you.* This is a worthy goal. It will provide the energy you need to make these all-important investments that we are about to discover.

> According to my earnest expectation and hope that in nothing I shall be ashamed, but with all boldness, as always, so now also Christ will be magnified in my body, whether by life or by death. For to me, to live *is* Christ, and to die *is* gain. (Philippians 1:20–21)

The right kind of investment will set you up for success in the future.

The Investments You Should Be Making

> Better is a poor man who walks in his integrity than a rich man who is crooked in his ways. (Proverbs 28:6, ESV)

Let's start with some questions I think everyone should be asking themselves. What areas of my life do I need to invest in right now? What will give me the most value and propel me toward being the very best that I can be?

Have you ever ventured into a new field of business without a guide or mentor? It can be unsettling. You are constantly wondering: Am I making the right decisions? Am I reading and understanding things properly? Is there some hidden secret that I need to know?

What if I told you that I have found the keys to success and a fulfilling life? Not only that, but these keys are proven, verifiable, and backed by the greatest bank and the most reliable government in the universe. Would you read further to find out what they are?

God, through His word, has provided precious and priceless insights for us so that we don't need to begin our journey by groping in the dark, trying out anything that comes along until we hopefully stumble into where we ought to be. God's word is our guide. It outlines for us the vital areas of life that will produce great results for anyone who dares to do what is required. It also provides a guarantee that the path outlined will never fail if it is followed. That's as bold a statement as I've ever heard. Let's see what it says in 2 Peter 1:1–11:

Simon Peter, a bondservant and apostle of Jesus Christ, to those who have obtained like precious faith with us by the righteousness of our God and Savior Jesus Christ:

Grace and peace be multiplied to you in the knowledge of God and of Jesus our Lord, as His divine power has given to us all things that *pertain* to life and godliness, through the knowledge of Him who called us by glory and virtue, by which have been given to us exceedingly great and precious promises, that through these you may be partakers of the divine nature, having escaped the corruption *that is* in the world through lust.

But also for this very reason, giving all diligence, add to your faith virtue, to virtue knowledge, to knowledge self-control, to self-control perseverance, to perseverance godliness, to godliness brotherly kindness, and to brotherly kindness love. For if these things are yours and abound, *you* will be neither barren nor unfruitful in the knowledge of our Lord Jesus Christ. For he who lacks these things is shortsighted, even to blindness, and has forgotten that he was cleansed from his old sins.

Therefore, brethren, be even more diligent to make your call and election sure, for if you do these things you will never stumble; for so an entrance will be supplied to you abundantly into the everlasting kingdom of our Lord and Savior Jesus Christ.

This passage lists a number of attributes that are vital for a rich, purposeful, and fulfilling life. They are faith, virtue, knowledge, self-control, perseverance, godliness, brotherly kindness, and love. These attributes can be further categorized into the three areas of vital importance that each of us need to invest in. They are:

1. Your relationship with God—faith, knowledge, godliness
2. Your character—virtue, self-control, perseverance, and godliness
3. Your relationship with others—brotherly kindness and love

When God gives you a guarantee, then there is absolutely no reason to worry or fret, because His word is good. When people or even organizations give you a guarantee, you should carefully consider whether they have the ability and resources to do what they've promised.

Years ago, I was deceived into believing a false warranty an attendant in the jewelry section of a store that has since closed gave me. The warranty was that a necklace I bought as a gift to my sister would never lose its luster or shine. The warranty information was outlined in a certificate that included a number to call if there were any issues and a contact address. It proved to be a worthless piece of paper. About a couple of years later, the store went out of business. I had completely forgotten about the jewelry until my sister called, complaining that the necklace was all dark and washed out. She wanted to follow up on the company's guarantee. Unfortunately, the store didn't exist anymore. Of what value, then, was their guarantee?

God's word is different. It lives and abides forever. There is nothing beyond the scope of its ability to change and influence—it is sharper than a two-edged sword. This is why you can be confident that what it promised will be accomplished. So what does the word of God say about making these investments in yourself? It says, "if you do these things you will never stumble," and you will be able to access the abundant benefits of the kingdom of our Lord Jesus Christ. That is a solid guarantee!

What Is Required?

Before we get into the details of each of these investments, there are important characteristics and indicators that provide evidence of your progress. We will use these as measures of how we are doing as we proceed. They are diligence and growth.

Diligence

Diligence is the continuous application of focused effort. This is not just activity or brawn, but effort that is focused on a specific area at a specific time in order to achieve desired changes. Can we measure diligence? Probably not quantitatively, but it can be measured by your ability to follow through and persist. It will be reflective of how much you continue to adhere to the outlined plan of action. Am I disciplined in my devotion of time? Am I following through with the action plan? These questions will easily reveal your level of diligence. "Work hard and become a leader; be lazy and become a slave" (Proverbs 12:24, NLT).

Growth

Growth is progress, and progress can be measurable and is evident. It is a positive change and improvement. An open and frank, but gentle periodic self-assessment is necessary to determine progress.

Without the application of these measures, the potential of what you can attain through the use of this book may not be realized.

Chapter 3

INVESTING IN YOUR RELATIONSHIP WITH GOD

GOD CRAVES A VIBRANT PERSONAL RELATIONSHIP WITH YOU. THE whole reason God created man was relationships. From the book of Genesis to Revelation, the Bible reveals God constantly at work to draw humanity back to Himself. Every blessing, rebuke, or correction is done with love for the same ultimate goal: that man may walk in continuous and close fellowship (communion) with God.

Relationship Determines Access

During the 2016 presidential election campaign in the United States, Hillary Clinton was repeatedly attacked by many about how the Clinton Foundation seemed to have leveraged their relationship with her to grant some donors access to her while she was Secretary of State. While there may or may not be some validity to their arguments, the truth that most would rather ignore is that relationship determines access. The better your relationship with someone, the more access you have to him or her.

Pastor E. A. Adeboye, the general overseer of the Redeemed Christian Church of God, talks about how when his children were very young, everyone knew that he was not to be disturbed whenever he was praying. However, the rule was repeatedly ignored by his children. They would come to him to ask whatever they needed. What gave them that confidence? It was relationship. Because he is their father, they were bold enough to approach him. God, our heavenly Father, would do the same and more. He desires that His children cultivate their relationship with Him and have unhindered access to all the goodness He has provided for them.

There are three important attributes that must be developed as part of the investment in your relationship with God. These attributes are faith, knowledge, and godliness.

Growing Your Faith Is an Investment in Your Relationship with God

Your faith is like a seed that requires careful attention, but when it blossoms, it becomes the source of an unending supply of good things. Faith is the foundation for membership in God's family. Two passages from the Bible help to buttress this point.

> For by grace you have been saved through faith, and that not of yourselves; *it is* the gift of God. (Ephesians 2:8)

> But without faith *it is* impossible to please *Him*, for he who comes to God must believe that He is,

and *that* He is a rewarder of those who diligently seek Him. (Hebrews 11:6)

Faith is the basis of the Christian's walk with God. Without faith, there is no access to God or relationship with Him. Grace works where there is faith.

Most people tend to have a good appreciation of the importance of money in their daily lives. Gold today (as it has been for many years now) is still the denominator of the value of a nation's currency and wealth. No matter where you go in the world, if you have lots of gold, you will still likely be considered wealthy. The Bible uses gold to describe the preciousness of our faith. It says our faith is "more precious than gold." As gold is a means of exchange in our world today, faith is also like a currency—the legal tender or means of transactional exchange in God's kingdom. Hebrews chapter 11 repeatedly uses the phrase "by faith." Many things were obtained through faith by the men and women referenced in that chapter.

When you grow your faith, you are growing your spiritual deposits and the ability to make significant spiritual transactions. Growing in faith enables you to enjoy the fullness of life available in Christ Jesus. The extent to which a believer can enjoy the benefits that are in Christ Jesus is determined by the level of his or her faith. The Bible says, "the just shall live by faith." This means:

- You can only enjoy the blessings of God in your life by your faith.
- Your faith will determine what you can receive from the Lord.
- You will experience the abundant life available in Christ by faith alone.

- You will make progress in your life by your faith.

How Can I Grow My Faith?

"Faith begins where the will of God is known" (Kenneth E. Hagin). God's will is revealed through His word. The Bible, which is God's word, clearly reveals God's desires, plans, and purposes for humanity. As we turn to those words, know them, study, and apply them in our lives, faith germinates and flourishes just as Romans 10:17 says: faith comes by hearing the word of God.

There are many valuable teachings and resources available that can show you how to acquire the word of God for yourself. Numerous free resources are available online and can be easily found by using your favorite search engine. Growth in faith is impossible without a commitment to acquiring the word. Spiritual growth is limited and stunted without a serious personal commitment to the discipline of learning the word of God. Let's look at a few helpful insights into how to grow your faith.

Acquire and Live by the Word

How do you acquire the word of God? You get God's word into you by listening to it, reading, studying, memorizing, and meditating on it. Technology has made the scripture readily available to almost anyone who desires it and has unfettered Internet access. There are also free Bible apps available for download on smart phones that provide audio, text, and study resources. Lack of access to resources is longer an excuse for many of us.

An easy way to get into hearing and reading the word of God is to incorporate it into your daily schedule. Make reading a portion of scripture a part of your daily time of devotion and listen to it while working out in the gym, at home, or when you're out for a walk. The more you incorporate reading and hearing into your daily schedule, the easier and more natural the process becomes.

Meditating is the process of reflecting on what you have heard or read. It is simply focusing your mind and thought on the word and contemplating what it means and how it applies to you. You can meditate on the word anytime. It may be in a quiet, secluded area or in a noisy, public place; anywhere will work as long as you can focus your mind on the word, even if only for a few minutes at a time.

Memorizing is a more deliberate process that may take different forms for different people. I find it easy to memorize when I write out the verse or text, read it to myself, and create a mental picture of the text. Repetition helps with memorization. Find a process that works for you. The goal is to make learning the word of God part of your regular schedule and to maximize your retention of what you have learned.

After hearing, reading, studying, memorizing, and meditating on the word, what should you do with it? Apply it. Live by what it says and put it into practice in your life. You may begin this by asking the question, how does this apply to me? Is there something for me to do as a result? To believe God's word is to act on it. Jesus said, "All things are possible to him who believes." This implies that all things are possible for him who receives the word of God and does what it says.

Exercise Your Faith Muscles

How can I exercise faith muscles? The Bible says that to build my faith, I must continuously feed on the word of God. That means I must continue in the practices that will help acquire and retain the word of God in my mind, in my heart, and in my mouth (Joshua 1:8; Romans 10:17). The word that is acquired needs to be applied in my life.

I love to eat steak. For me, good steak must be prepared "medium well plus." That is, well done without being burnt. Despite how much I love to eat steak—or any other food, for that matter—I have realized that the more I eat, the more work I need to do in order to convert the food into useful energy and get rid of the excess calories.

Just as a person who continually eats without exercising becomes fat and potentially unhealthy, the person who acquires the word but does nothing with it is spiritually unhealthy. Exercising my faith muscles is putting God's word into practice in my life.

How can you exercise your faith? You do this by:

- Practicing and acting on the word.
- Stretching yourself in faith. Get out of your comfort zone and do things the word of God says you can and should be doing. Tell someone about God's love. Pray for or with someone in faith, expecting the release of God's power into the situation.
- Obeying God's word without hesitation.
- Walking in love.
- Praying in the Spirit and with the Holy Spirit's help.

- Giving praise and glory to the Lord.

Growing in the Knowledge of God

Our world today thrives on the continuous acquisition of knowledge. There is so much more information and knowledge available and easily accessible to almost anyone today than was dreamed feasible a few decades ago. This increase in knowledge has led to significant advancements in medicine, science, and technology.

Unfortunately, as knowledge has increased in these areas, there has been a progressive decline in the desire for the knowledge of God. The Bible clearly warns that this will happen: "Iniquity shall abound and the love of men shall wax cold." This should not be the case for those who want to maximize their God-given potential. For these, there must be a realization of their need for God and a personal commitment to seek to know him better. Like the Apostle Paul, their singular passion must be "that I may know Him."

A diligent pursuit of God is accomplished through the study of the word of God, prayer, and worship. "Be diligent to present yourself approved to God, a worker who does not need to be ashamed, rightly dividing the word of truth" (2 Timothy 2:15).

Growing in Godliness

Godliness is a quality that is easily misunderstood but is a necessity for anyone desirous of a vibrant relationship with God our Father. It is the quality that differentiates between those who are truly committed to walking with the Lord and those who merely pay lip service to the idea. To the latter, it is just an idea, a generalization, and a wish, but to those who really want to walk with Him, it is a necessity and an inviolable commitment of their daily lives.

Godliness can be described as being fit for divine purposes. It is the process of imitating God (god-like-ness), and becoming more and more like Him. Another definition of godliness is spiritual training. We will be devoting some time to understanding what this implies and how it should mold our daily lives.

Growth in godliness is God's objective for every one of His children. The result of the process is becoming like Christ (Romans 8:29).

Godliness Does Not Have to Be Boring

The idea of godliness evokes a picture in the modern mind that is akin to a boring, repetitive lifestyle that is archaic, almost impossible to do, and not to be desired. That imagery has its foundation in the teachings and practices over many decades that equate godliness and holiness with fun-less, lackluster, and joyless living. That couldn't be any further from the truth.

Rather than being dull, godliness is fun. Fun does not have to be sinful. Can I have lots of fun without sinning? Certainly! Jesus Christ went to a party, yet was (and still is) an embodiment of godliness. Undoubtedly, you would have seen or heard of a little girl who was imitating her mother or the little boy who imagined he was his dad and imitated him. Do you think that was painful to the child? Definitely not. It was fun—something to be enjoyed, imagined, and practiced. You probably were that child some time ago. That is what godliness is like. It is imitating God, your Father. It can be lots of fun if you will make it so. "Therefore be imitators of God as dear children" (Ephesians 5:1).

Godliness Is Profitable

As I grow older, I have become more discerning about how I spend my time. Though I love to relax and do nothing sometimes, the reality of the scarcity of time seems to be more poignant to me now than ever before. I would rather not spend time on things or with people that will not add value to me, because time is life. When you waste it, you waste life. Similarly, investing in godliness makes sense because it adds value to you. "For physical training is of some value, but godliness has value for all things, holding promise for both the present life and the life to come. [9] This is a trustworthy saying that deserves full acceptance" (1 Timothy 4:8–9, NIV).

Imagine you are a stock market enthusiast, who has some funds available for investment, and you have found a stock with a great upside. It is well managed, with a great history of consistent growth and significant positive yield, and very little risk. Will you invest in it? I certainly would. A continuous investment in godliness has great upsides with very little risk and an immense potential to never stop yielding positive fruits for you.

Elements of Godliness

There are certain essential traits you will see in a son imitating his father or in the little girl pretending to be her mom. They are:

- Love for the parent,

- The desire to spend time with the parent, and
- Practicing being or imitating the parent.

These traits apply to godliness as well, but to an even greater degree. Cultivating your love for God your Father is the first and necessary step for godliness. I would not want to be like Him unless I loved Him and everything about Him. The more I love Him, the more I will want to be with Him and like Him. This explains why the greatest commandment is "You shall love the Lord your God with all your heart, with all your soul, and with all your mind" (Matthew 22:36–38).

In Psalm 63, David presented us with a practical example of how to invest in your relationship with God. He cultivated the habits that endeared God (our Father) to his heart and enabled growth in godliness. David demonstrated what we have identified as the essential traits of godliness.

In the next chapter, we will be examining how you can cultivate these habits and grow in intimacy with God. Before then, I want to encourage you to make David's words yours. Think about them for a moment. Do they describe your relationship with God? Do they reflect the state of your heart right now, or do they sound like an ideal, a concept that is a little far out, but something that you hope someday will describe your walk with God? Making this a reality in your life is what investing in yourself is about.

Read these words out loud to yourself:

O God, You are my God; early will I seek You;
my soul thirsts for You; my flesh longs for You

in a dry and thirsty land where there is no water. So I have looked for You in the sanctuary, to see Your power and Your glory. Because Your loving kindness is better than life, my lips shall praise You. Thus I will bless You while I live; I will lift up my hands in Your name. My soul shall be satisfied as with marrow and fatness, and my mouth shall praise You with joyful lips. When I remember You on my bed, I meditate on You in the night watches. Because You have been my help, therefore in the shadow of Your wings I will rejoice. My soul follows close behind You; Your right hand upholds me. (Psalm 63:1–8)

Chapter 4

THE PRACTICE OF GODLINESS

"Exercise to stimulate, not to annihilate. The world wasn't formed in a day, and neither were we. Set small goals and build upon them." Lee Haney

SIMONE BILES IS A REMARKABLE OLYMPIAN ATHLETE WHO REPRE-sented the United States in gymnastics at the 2016 Olympics in Rio, Brazil. Many ardent followers of the sport predicted that she was going to win multiple medals because of her talent and how she was significantly better than a lot of her contemporaries. She proved them right and validated their confidence in her abilities. How did she achieve this?

Simone, like a lot of other Olympic athletes, devoted her life to the sport. It was her consuming passion, her purpose, and the primary determinant of how everything else was prioritized—where she lived, the schools she attended, who trained her, and so on. Her vision to be an Olympian drove her into what is so far a lifelong commitment to training and discipline.[1]

Simone was born on March 14, 1997, in Columbus, Ohio. She and her sister, Adria, were raised by their grandfather and grandmother, Ron and Nellie. At the tender age of six, she was introduced to gymnastics when she visited a gymnastics center on a field trip from a day care. Then began what has become for her a lifelong quest of training and developing her skills until now, at the age of nineteen, she is the most decorated American gymnast in history.

Benjamin Franklin is credited with coining the saying that there are no gains without pains. Many people would love to have the accolades and fame and achieve the successes of Simone Biles, but how many are willing to pay the price of thirteen years of continued, ardent devotion and discipline?

The inescapability of the choice we have to make was succinctly captured by Jim Rohn when he said, "We must all suffer from one of two pains: the pain of discipline or the pain of regret. The difference is discipline weighs ounces while regret weighs tons."[2]

Would you choose the path and pain of discipline, or would you rather do nothing until the weight of the pain of regret settles in?

Godliness is Spiritual Training

> For physical training is of some value, but godliness (spiritual training) is of value in everything *and* in every way, since it holds promise for the present life and for the life to come. This is a faithful *and* trustworthy saying worthy of full acceptance *and* approval. (1 Timothy 4:8–9, AMP)

Godliness is the process of developing the habits and disciplines that enable you to become more aware and attuned to who you are in Christ. It is the process that propels your spiritual growth and prepares you for the plans and purposes of God for your life. It will draw you closer to the Lord and train your inner being to be vibrant, sensitive, and alive to God.

Just as certain disciplines are needed for an athlete to achieve success and reach the epitome of his or her sport, there are also spiritual disciplines for success. Developing and mastering these spiritual disciplines is as important as (if not even more significant than) the physical disciplines and exercises.

The Discipline of Prayer

Prayer is an exercise that every Christian should practice and thrive in. Prayer becomes a challenge when we build structures and rules into it outside of the fundamentals of what is necessary to make it effective.

Even a little one-year-old child prays. Prayer is communication. For us, it is communication with God our Father. The believer's prayer is not some dull, difficult activity, but a fun-filled, two-way activity that builds your spirit, strengthens you, and enhances the quality of your life.

Prayer becomes a discipline when it goes beyond the casual thing you do whenever you remember or as a last resort in an emergency and becomes a daily, methodical, deliberate activity you embark upon.

So how do I make prayer into a discipline? The first thing is to enjoy praying. What are those things that bring smiles to your face? The thoughts of your children or grandchildren, a situation that the Lord brought you through, or a word that someone shared with you? What is it for you? Start by talking to God about these things. In doing so, you're not asking for anything but cultivating a habit of gratitude and appreciation for the blessings of the Lord in your life. Like the Psalmist said, "O that men would praise the Lord for His goodness and His wonderful works."

Start with what brings a smile to your face. A joyful heart is a heart that is primed for worship. You will soon realize that every time you begin like this in prayer, you will become so engrossed in worship and thanksgiving that other things will begin to pale in significance. Worship from a joyful heart.

Our Lord Jesus Christ provided us with what we can use as a model for prayer in Matthew 6. Though it is not my intention to elucidate on the dynamics of prayer in this writing, I believe it's important to point out some of what makes for an effective prayer to God. These include:

1. An acknowledgement of God as your Father
2. Worship and veneration of His greatness and majesty
3. A commitment to His purpose and will
4. A personal consecration and dedication
5. A specific request for what you desire in your life in accordance with His word
6. Confidence and boldness in coming before Him, with the assurance that He hears you
7. Expectation

The next step in developing the discipline of prayer is to cultivate a prayer model that works for you and that utilizes the gifting and grace that God has bestowed on you.

One of the many tendencies in full gospel circles today is the inclination to believe that a prayer is not effective until it is said in a certain way and probably repeated a number of times. God is not hard of hearing. He is certainly not deaf. There are times when it may be appropriate or natural to shout, scream, and jump in prayer, but certainly not when I am talking to my Father. I will raise my voice, shout, or even do more if I address the devil or some of his works. When I go before my Heavenly Father, I want to sing to Him, talk to Him gently, and appreciate Him. This has become the model for me. The model works for me because I love music, and I am convinced that God created me just to worship Him. So what do I do?

I sing to Him in my understanding (that is, in all the languages that I understand), and I sing to Him in the spirit (1 Corinthians 14:15). Will that work for you? Certainly, if you cultivate the habit. However, and more importantly, you should leverage the abilities that God has given to you.

If you love to write poems and inspirational thoughts, why not write something for your Heavenly Father? You can read the note to Him every day to start your prayer session until you're inspired to write more. You don't need to share the writing with anyone else. It's just between you and Him. Make it your love letter to God. That way, you're not necessarily concerned about the form or quality of the writing. You just do it—from you to Him, from your heart to His. That is the kind of genuineness of fellowship God desires.

The third step in developing the discipline of prayer is to find a time and place that works for you. It may be your lunch time at work, or it may be in the evening when you take a walk in your neighborhood. It may be in the early hours of the day, before everyone else rises. Determine what works best for you, and stick with it. The important thing is to do it repeatedly and continuously—at the same time and in the same place as much as possible.

We are creatures of habit. The habits we form mold our lives and determine our futures. A habit of prayer will make you strong in the Lord and prepare you to handle the vagaries of life. "Be strong in the Lord and in the power of His might." Strength comes when we wait on the Lord diligently and consistently. "They that wait upon the Lord shall renew their strength" (Isaiah 40:31, KJV).

The fourth step to cultivating the discipline of prayer is to monitor the time you spend in focused prayer with the intention of gradually growing to a level you can sustain. Time yourself. Start with a reasonable goal—say fifteen minutes—and periodically stretch yourself in five-minute increments until you reach your desired objective for a daily time of prayer.

There is no hard and fast rule about how much time is appropriate. What really counts is the quality of the time and the consistency. If your goal is thirty minutes daily, great. Do it. Start small and continue to grow until you attain your goal. Allow yourself room to grow.

Your time of fellowship and communion with God can be varied, refreshing, and fun. You can make it so through what you do during the period.

Train yourself to pray. Like I stated earlier, prayer is natural, and natural skills can be enhanced through practice. You can train yourself in prayer by doing a number of things:

1. Develop a list of things to pray for—weekly, monthly, or even daily.

    Your list helps guide you as you pray, but it also allows you to keep track of those things that God has done in answer to your prayers. They will become your list of testimonies because God answers prayers.

2. Develop a list of scriptures that focus on some of God's attributes or characteristics, like His greatness, faithfulness, and abilities. Use these scriptures as your foundation for prayers. Some of my favorites are Psalms 91, 103, and 145. Psalm 103 begins with *"Bless the Lord, O my soul and all that is within me, bless His holy name!"* This always stirs up praise in my heart. It's my trigger scripture to praise and celebrate all the Lord has done for me. Find one that does the same (and more) for you. Use it repeatedly until it becomes a habit.

The Discipline of Worship

Worship flows out of a heart in love with God. Cultivating the discipline of worship is cultivating your love for God.

The reference to worship stirs up different mental images in people. For some, it's a picture of quietly kneeling down behind a pew and contemplating the greatness of God in your heart. For others, it's singing, dancing, and exuberance in praise and thanksgiving. These mental images do depict worship in some sense, but worship is much more. Worship is *living* every moment in honor and adoration of the Lord because He is worth it. Worship is a life committed to God's pleasure and will. The heart of the worshipper says, "I live to please you, Lord."

"Take your everyday, ordinary life—your sleeping, eating, going-to-work, and walking-around life—and place it before God as an offering" (Romans 12:1, MSG). The worship of God is giving your life as an offering to Him.

So how do I develop the discipline of worship? Developing the discipline of worship begins with an understanding of what being an "offering to the Lord" means. It means everything about you is on the altar of worship; all of you belongs to Him. Now that's an easy statement to make, but a seemingly tough thing to do when one doesn't understand what it means. It means pleasing God comes before pleasing myself. It also means sticking to my commitment to please the Lord despite whatever the personal cost may be to me. It means living holy—every day.

The following is a list of certain things that will flow from a life committed to loving the Lord.

- Spend time with Him.
- Live for Him alone.
- Seek to please Him continually.
- Praise Him, and always tell Him how good He is and declare the greatness of His power.
- Evaluate yourself to determine that there's nothing you are withholding from the altar of worship. Is there an area of your life that is still difficult to let go of? Is there someone

you're struggling to forgive? The discipline of worship demands forgiveness and total surrender to God.

The Discipline of Studying God's Word

A young man was once told by a very wise sage who knew the secrets of success, fulfillment, and purposeful living that if he would pay attention to the words in a book, his success in life was guaranteed. The young man dutifully followed the sage's advice. He studied and memorized the contents of the book and practiced its teachings diligently. Sure enough, as promised, he became very successful. At the time of his death at a very old age, the young man, now old, had achieved some of the greatest feats in human history. He became one of the greatest generals of his time and also became what we would refer to today as the president and commander-in-chief of his nation. He led his nation through a challenging period of conquests and resettlement. He also developed a generation of leaders who were able to continue the work of leading the nation after him.

If you had the same opportunity, would you follow the sage's advice and do what the young man did? I believe you have the opportunity today, just like this man did centuries ago. The man was Joshua. God—the all-knowing and all-wise God—told him:

> This Book of the Law shall not depart from your mouth, but you shall read [and meditate on] it day and night, so that you may be careful to do [everything] in accordance with all that is written in it;

for then you will make your way prosperous, and
then you will be successful. (Joshua 1:8, AMP)

God's words to Joshua form the template for the discipline of
studying the Bible—God's word. The instruction to Joshua was:

SPEAK

Constantly talk about God's word to yourself and to all others
who will listen to you or follow you. In today's parlance, speak, write,
tweet, and blog about the word of God.

READ

Read it every day—day or night.

MEDITATE

Think on it. Ruminate, muse, and reflect on the word of God.
The questions to ask yourself during your time of reflection include:
What does it mean to me? What is God saying specifically to me
through the text? Is there something I need to change? Is there an
instruction I need to obey?

APPLY

Practice it. Live by the word of God. Do what is says to do. The
Bible is God's instruction for life, so live by it.

All Scripture *is* given by inspiration of God, and *is* profitable for doctrine, for reproof, for correction, for instruction in righteousness, that the man of God may be complete, thoroughly equipped for every good work. (2 Timothy 3:16–17)

How do I develop the discipline of speaking and studying God's word? Read it out loud to yourself. Memorize at least one verse a week. Repeat the process of memorization until you know the particular scripture perfectly. Write out verses on specific promises of God that you want to claim. Take them along with you everywhere. Memorize these and use them as a foundation for your prayers. Obey and follow fully all the precepts for life clearly stated in God's word. If you need clarity on an issue, search the scriptures, pray for understanding, and seek godly counsel.

The Discipline of Fasting

If you are like me, the first thought that would probably come to your mind at this point is, show me where it says in the Bible that I must fast in order to grow spiritually and succeed in God's purpose for my life. Well, the Bible didn't explicitly say so, but Jesus said that after He is taken up, His disciples (which are you and me) will fast and pray because the dynamics will be different (Mark 2:19–20). These are those days.

We don't fast to lose weight or just for survival. The believer in Christ needs to fast and pray to grow, take new ground, and advance spiritually and physically. Our warfare—battles and conflicts—are not rooted in the physical. They are spiritual. Spiritual battles demand spiritual weaponry.

The Bible is replete with examples of men and women who practiced this discipline. What will this discipline achieve for you?

- It will prepare you for the seasons and tasks ahead of you.
- It will build, strengthen, and embolden your spirit man (inner man—the real you) when accompanied with fervent prayers.
- It will help consecrate and separate your body to God in holiness and purity.
- It will enhance effectiveness in the place of prayer.
- Fasting with prayer fans the flame of spiritual revival. It keeps the fire on your altar of worship.

How Do You Fast?

Outline a purpose for your fast. Is it personal growth, tackling a particular issue or challenge, quietness and reflection, or another reason? Your purpose determines what you do during the fast. All fasts are not alike.

Prepare yourself physically and spiritually. Avoid overextending yourself physically before commencing a fast. Identify a scriptural foundation and theme for your fast. If fasting for an extended period of time, keep a prayer journal or use a guide that will help you to stay focused on the goal of your fast.

Make fasting a habit by doing it regularly if possible. The frequency depends on your goal. It could be monthly, biweekly, or even weekly as the need warrants. It's important for every believer who desires to grow in the Lord to carve out some time periodically for solitude, reflection, and waiting on the Lord. It may be difficult to start, but it becomes easier with time when there is a definite purpose and goal defined for it.

The Discipline of Sharing Christ

Sharing Christ does not have to be a laborious and difficult task. We share Christ through the lives we live daily. As disciples and followers of Christ, we are called to represent Him, show His love, and demonstrate His power. We do not do these only within the confines of our church assemblies, but on the streets, in our homes, at our jobs, and everywhere we go. You are the light of the world that is designed by God not to be hidden but to be seen. We are the text of the living gospel of Christ to be seen and read by people everywhere.

Cultivating this habit begins with a little self-adjustment. The following are a few proven tips that will help you along this path:

- Develop a genuine interest in people. Listen to them, be interested in them and where they are in life, and show it.
- When the opportunity avails itself, ask questions. Ask about their welfare. Ask about the things you've talked about with the person in the past if you've previously engaged them in a conversation. Show genuine care. Pretense can be easily detected.
- Offer to pray with people whenever possible.
- Share how the Lord has helped you or someone else you know through a similar situation if applicable. Go soft on being preachy.

- Offer hope through Christ. Hope and forgiveness are not common qualities in the world without Jesus Christ. Our mandate as believers is to carry this message of hope, forgiveness, love, and reconciliation to our world.

In cultivating this discipline, we must realize that it is our responsibility as believers to share Christ with our world. Christ will not come and do it. The angels are not called to do so. It is our responsibility alone, and we must do it with every opportunity and ounce of strength that we have. Jesus said we are the salt of the earth and the light of the world. Our duty and charge is to make a difference in the lives around us, starting with our immediate families.

The Discipline of Loving Others

"By this all will know that you are My disciples, if you have love for one another" (John 13:35). Genuine love is the hallmark of Christianity. Faith is void and of no value when there is no love. Cultivating the habit of loving others should come easily and naturally to anyone whose heart is surrendered to Christ. Why is this so?

Man is a tripartite being. He is first a spirit, with a soul (the seat of the intellect, mind, and emotions), living in a physical body. When a person surrenders to the Lord and asks him into his or her life, the first thing that happens is a regeneration of the inner or spirit man. The spirit man, which was previously dead and separated from God due to sin (Genesis 3), is renewed and born again. It becomes alive to God and then takes on the nature of God—God's DNA. God is love. That is His nature and DNA. A born-again believer automatically receives this nature, regardless of whether they feel like it or not.

With the transformation that takes place at the new birth comes the grace and capacity to love like God. It is, however, important to note that though my spirit man is renewed, my mind—thoughts, emotions, intellect, and so forth—is not. The process of renewing the mind begins when I start to get hold of the word of God and live by it.

God's deposit of love in my inner being needs to be cultivated—nurtured, fed, and strengthened—until it permeates every area of my life. One habit that I've stumbled into that has helped me significantly in the area of loving others—beginning with Christians (church members) and then everyone else—is telling myself that I love everyone. I've found that doing so has an unusual and powerful attitude-changing and mindset-changing effect for me. I believe it will help you as well, because we become what we say.

Many times while driving, I would say out loud to myself again and again, "I love everyone!" The first time I did this was while consumed with the pain and disappointment that sometimes come with relating and interacting with people. The more I thought about the situations, the gloomier I became, until the Holy Spirit stirred those words into my heart. Uttering them ushered in a glow and peace into my heart that surprised me, and it immediately changed the state of my heart. Instead of gloom, worry, concern, and disappointment, a sense of joy, peace, and love began to overwhelm me, and I couldn't help but say it out louder: I love everyone!

God is love. He wants His children to love like Him regardless of what others do or refuse to do. Love anyway and love always.

That's the disciple's standard. Invest time and effort into developing the discipline of loving others. The benefits are transformational, tangible, and eternal. The following are steps to take that will set you on the path to developing this discipline.

- Act Like You Would If You Loved Someone
  Love must be in word and action.
- Resolve to Forgive

  Forgiveness is as necessary for love as air is for life. Resolving to forgive is a decision to take whatever steps are necessary "as long as it depends on you" (Romans 12:18, NIV) to settle a matter and let it go. You need to first let go in your mind before attempting to talk it out or work through the problem with the other party—whoever did the wrong. Forgiveness is your decision and does not need to be predicated on what the other person does or doesn't do. Love anyway, and love always. Forgive anyway, and forgive always! "If you forgive others the wrongs they have done to you, your Father in heaven will also forgive you" (Matthew 6:14, GNT). The Message paraphrase translates the text this way: "In prayer there is a connection between what God does and what you do. You can't get forgiveness from God, for instance, without forgiving others. If you refuse to do your part, you cut yourself off from God's part." Resolve to forgive quickly. If you delay, you are delaying your blessings from God.

- Practice Giving
  Love gives. It is impossible to love without giving. Give to God and give to people.

The Discipline of Abstinence

Many people will tell you that abstinence is not only impossible in today's world, but that it is mean and unrealistic to set or have that expectation for anyone. I disagree. No matter how common and widely acceptable even among "Christians" this kind of thinking has become, it is untrue. Abstinence is possible, realistic, and achievable by anyone who chooses to commit to what is required.

Our heavenly Father is not mean, difficult, or unrealistic in His expectations. He will not ask anyone to do anything if He has not already supplied them with the grace and ability to do it. One of my favorite Bible passages affirms this truth:

> No temptation [regardless of its source] has over-
> taken *or* enticed you that is not common to human
> experience [nor is any temptation unusual or
> beyond human resistance]; but God is faithful [to
> His word—He is compassionate and trustworthy],
> and He will not let you be tempted beyond your
> ability [to resist], but along with the temptation
> He [has in the past and is now and] will [always]

provide the way out as well, so that you will be able to endure it [without yielding, and will overcome temptation with joy]. (1 Corinthians 10:13, AMP)

What are we to abstain from? Abstain from every form of evil (1 Thessalonians 5:22). Anything that dishonors God is evil. Anything that taints our testimony of faith in the Lord is evil. Anything that is contrary to God's word and His revealed purpose is evil.

As you begin to think about this description of what is evil, you will realize that many things we do and take for granted daily easily fall into this category. The questions to ask yourself are: Does this habit, choice, desire, or whatever it may be honor God? Will the Lord be pleased with me as I engage in it? Anything that I am unable to do with a sense of confidence (i.e., faith), though I have the legal right to do so, is sin.

You may say, but God doesn't want us to be bound by rules— don't touch this or don't do that. In a sense you will be right, but the whole truth is that Christ freed us from the bondage of rules and regulations so that we can live by a higher law: the law of love. The law of love frees us to live holy, not just out of an obligation or fear, but because we love Him and desire to please Him in all we do.

So how do you develop the discipline of abstinence?

1. Make pleasing God your daily goal.
2. Identify the areas of your life that you need to pay close attention to.

   Develop safeguards and reminders that will propel you toward your dedication to God. The fact that you have struggled in the past does not mean discipline and abstinence is out of reach. Ask the Lord for help.

3. Win each day.

   The goal of abstinence is pursued one day at a time. It should be a daily consecration. When you focus your mind on winning today, that is, abstaining just today from the things that easily trip you up, it will be easier to win. Each day is a new opportunity to refocus, stand on God's word, rededicate yourself to Him, and resist temptations.

4. Resist temptations firmly.

   The Bible says to resist steadfastly in your faith. Stand firm against temptation, be strong in your faith, and know that you are not alone in the battle. Other Christians are going through the same challenges as you are, and the Lord has promised to make His grace available for every test and lead you to victory. Remember that you only need to resist today. Each day of victory makes you stronger, surer, and more able to say no when next it comes your way.

5. Extricate yourself from the situations, places, or relationships that create the opportunities for the temptations. "Do not be deceived: 'Evil company corrupts good habits.'" (1 Corinthians 15:33)

6. Be open about your struggles, commitment, and goals. Find a friend that you can be accountable to who can challenge you, or better still, you can challenge each other to be better and stronger and hold yourselves accountable to keeping your commitments to the Lord.

7. Trust the Lord for grace each day.

Make requesting His grace for each day part of your daily routine. Avoid starting your day without asking for and receiving, by faith, the grace you will need.

8. Celebrate every single day of abstinence and victory. Being conscious of what the Lord has done and appreciating and celebrating Him and yourself strengthens you for the days ahead. It will prepare you for the next victory. You can do it. You were created by God to win in every battle of life. His grace is available and will be abundantly supplied to you.

The Discipline of Committed Service

As a steward of God's grace, I must use the talents, abilities, and resources He has given me in a way that pleases and glorifies Him. There's no room for idleness in God's kingdom. Anyone who will walk with the Lord must be willing and available for any purpose He may need fulfilled. God formed you uniquely, so you could serve Him (Ephesians 2:10). Our tendency is to wait for the grand assignment or task while God is waiting on us to be faithful and serve Him diligently where we are now.

Opportunities for service abound in your local church and community. Don't wait or sit idle. Get involved now. How do you start?

1. Get involved in your local church. Don't wait for a special calling. Volunteer for any available task and do it well as unto the Lord.

2. Join a service group in your church. Joining a service group helps to develop accountability and aligns your service with the needs of the organization.

3. Pray for opportunities to serve God and others as the Lord would have you to. Pray that you will be a fruitful and faithful steward of God's grace on your life.

4. Serve others by telling them about Jesus.

5. Periodically review what you have done in serving others. Some questions you may ask yourself are: Am I serving to the best of my ability? Are my motives for service right? Why am I doing this? Can I do more? Is there something I could do differently? Are there other areas where I could be of service?

Notes

1. Wikipedia contributors, "Simone Biles," *Wikipedia, The Free Encyclopedia,* https://en.wikipedia.org/w/index.php?title=Simone_Biles&oldid=782729183 (accessed March 22, 2017).

2. Anthony St. Peter, *The Greatest Quotations of All-Time* (Xlibris Corporation, 2010); 530.

Goals

Vision Priorities

Persistence Purpose

Character

SurrenderToGod

SayNo

Chapter 5

INVESTING IN YOUR CHARACTER

Sow a thought, and you reap an act;
Sow an act, and you reap a habit;
Sow a habit, and you reap a character;
Sow a character, and you reap a destiny.
Samuel Smiles

I HAD A COLLEGE CLASSMATE WHO HAD A REPUTATION FOR BEING A "natural liar." It was almost impossible for anyone in the class to believe anything he said because of his great inclination to lie. Literally, the first words out of his mouth in most situations were lies. If you unwittingly asked him what time it was and he answered, you had better confirm his answer with someone else, or you could end up in a mess if you relied just on his word. Have you ever met someone like that? The problem is a flawed character. It may be masked as a tendency to be playful, but it's much more. To make matters worse for this former classmate, he got into a so-called modern-day religion known as Eckankar. Sadly, it only made him worse.

Unfortunately for him, Eckankar did nothing to change or improve his character; rather, he became worse.

The Bible says that a person speaks out of the abundance of what is in his heart. It is an undeniable truth that no matter how much you try, you can only give out of what's in you. A flawed character will definitely manifest itself, no matter how much one tries to cover up. True and lasting transformation begins with submission to the word of God and the work of the Holy Spirit.

What's the Big Deal about Character?

Your character is a window to your soul. A good, healthy character reveals an inner being that is growing and progressively being transformed into the image and nature of Christ. There are a few things in life that are completely indifferent to your race, background, or upbringing but have a powerful influence on what you can become. A godly character is one of them.

There is a saying that birds of the same feather flock together. When a person is of great character, he or she will naturally attract individuals of similar character quality and disposition. Character differentiates a person who can be trusted from one who cannot be trusted. Organizations and businesses are constantly investing millions of dollars to seek people with admirable and needed character traits like integrity and honesty. They do so out of the proven belief that their organizations will be better positioned to thrive and succeed if they have such employees at every level. Integrity and honesty are key attributes of great leadership. No right-thinking person would depend on someone whose word is unreliable.

"Gain a modest reputation for being unreliable and you will never be asked to do a thing" (Paul Theroux). There are worse character traits and attributes than being called unreliable. However, all such negative traits, without exception, will lead a person down the path of regrets, loneliness, and wasted opportunities. An investment in building a great character is an investment in building a future filled with possibilities, growth, positive relationships, and meaningful partnerships. No one succeeds in life alone. A solid character enables you to align with the right people and attract favor, and prepares you for the rare opportunities of life.

Investing in developing a godly character:

- Ensures your place in the plans and purposes of God for your life,
- Will help you to fulfill your destiny,
- Will win you a good reputation before God and man,
- Will win you favor, and
- Will make you exceptional.

Habits form character. Developing godly habits will lead to the development of a godly character.

The Apostle Peter gives us some valuable clues about the character attributes we should develop. Some of these are virtue (integrity, goodness, respectability, and dignity), self-control (self-discipline, restraint, and composure), and perseverance (persistence, determination, tenacity, and staying power). How can we develop these traits?

The Lord sent us His Holy Spirit to help us. He is our Teacher and Guide. His indwelling presence causes His nature to be revealed in us, but we have a great part to play in doing the work to develop a godly character.

> But the fruit of the Spirit is love, joy, peace, long-suffering, kindness, goodness, faithfulness, gentleness, self-control. Against such there is no law. And those *who are* Christ's have crucified the flesh with its passions and desires. If we live in the Spirit, let us also walk in the Spirit. Let us not become conceited, provoking one another, envying one another. (Galatians 5:22–25)

Surrender to the Holy Spirit

To surrender to the Holy Spirit is a choice the believer has to make. It is a choice to give up control to God. This means I choose not to live as I feel or want, but to do as He says. This is the implication of walking in the spirit. "If we live in the Spirit, let us also walk in the Spirit."

How do we live in the spirit? By ceding control to God who indwells the believer and leads us in the path of His will to follow. Furthermore, you must:

- Acknowledge Him as your Teacher and Guide,
- Ask for Him to lead you each day, and
- Practice overflowing with the fruits of righteousness, which are love, joy, peace, kindness, goodness, faithfulness, gentleness, and self-control. Practice implies making the

conscious choice to do these things, such as choosing to be joyful instead of being sad.

There are a few things that I do to lift up my spirit and practice overflowing with the fruits of the Spirit. I believe that these will work for you as well.

1. Thank and praise the Lord for the blessing of each day.
2. Exercise your mind and body daily. I exercise my mind by meditating on the work of God and my body by spending at least thirty minutes each day walking, running, lifting, or swimming. A daily exercise of the mind and body will lift your spirit and enhance your attitude.
3. Listen to uplifting music. If you can, write a poem, a letter to God, or an uplifting letter to a friend. If so gifted, compose a song—your own song to God. Nobody else needs to know or hear it; it is just something between you and your God.
4. Eat a light meal with lots of fiber and protein. There are times to fast, but sometimes you just need a light, nutritious meal to get you in the right frame of mind.
5. Be a blessing to someone. Give someone a call. Show genuine care and bless them whichever way you can.
6. Smile. A smile is very therapeutic and highly infectious. It can change the atmosphere of a room and break through walls of depression. We need to smile and laugh more. "Rejoice in the Lord always. Again I will say, rejoice!"

The Holy Spirit in you guides and empowers you to live a joyful, victorious life. Consciously cultivating the habit of committing your day to Him and asking for direction are necessary steps in a life surrendered to God.

Purpose to Please

Purpose rules the world. The Bible tells us about how Daniel and his three friends became successful in an adverse situation when things were not ideal for them or going the way they had dreamed they would. They were slaves in Babylon, and through divine providence, had the unusual privilege of being selected as part of a very few to be schooled in the culture, traditions, and knowledge of the modern societies of their time. With this privilege came the opportunity to continually partake of the food from the king's table. Daniel and his friends, however, determined they would not eat of the food or drinks in order not to defile themselves before their God. Rather, they chose to eat lentils and drink water. They were determined to please the Lord, and He honored their dedication by making them exceptional in all matters in which they were tested.

Pleasing the Lord begins with an awareness of His omniscience and omnipresence. He knows all, sees all, and is everywhere. He is not many miles away in Israel, as some would have thought in this instance. He is ever so near to those who are His. As C. Austin Miles wrote in the old favorite song "In the Garden,"

> And He walks with me
> And He talks with me
> And He tells me I am His own

And the joy we share as we tarry there
None other has ever known.

Purpose to please the Lord. Make pleasing God your personal commitment. The Bible says it's only reasonable to do so in the light of all He has done for us and is to us (Romans 12:1).

Pleasing Him is a choice. It comes from a commitment of the heart to do only what He wants you to do. This determination and purpose of heart manifests in different ways. For instance, a married couple having a disagreement decides to sit down, talk through, and resolve their issues because God's word says not to let the sun go down on your anger. It is the same purpose of heart that makes a young lady or young man decide to keep themselves sexually pure until marriage (despite the temptations to do otherwise) because the Bible says that sex is for marriage. For another person, this determination to please the Lord may manifest in the decision to share with others and care for those in need because God is love.

Purposing to please the Lord is living for an audience of one. Who is that one? Will it be you—your desires, will, pleasures, goals, and feelings—or will it be God? Developing a godly character requires a commitment to please the Lord. Make that determination. Let it be your purpose and passion today.

Learning to Say No

Learning to say no to ourselves is one of the harder traits to develop. It is relatively easier to say no to someone who wants something from you than to say no to yourself. Though it can still be tough at times to say no to another person, depending on what it is or who it is asking, the greater challenge is denying yourself something you want that is easily within your reach.

You may be wondering, why do I need to deny myself anything? Our modern world questions the need for self-denial in many vital areas of life. The typical mindset is, "Do it if it feels good as long as it doesn't hurt anyone else." That is a mindset that promotes self-gratifying indiscipline over the tried and tested virtues of contentment and self-denial in order to advance a greater good and fulfill the divine purpose. Developing a Christian mindset is a must, and it begins with the questions: Will this be pleasing to the Lord? Will this action bring honor to God?

The farthest thing from most of us at the times when we are faced with conflicting options is the ability to engage in rational thought. Decisions are then mostly emotional and based on the anticipation of a certain form of gratification. The Bible offers a way out: "But I say, live by the Spirit and you will not carry out the desires of the flesh" (Galatians 5:16 NET Bible).

What this means is, if my life is daily surrendered to God, I would have positioned myself to continuously become stronger and able to say no to anything that would distract me from that devotion. In addition to this, we are also provided with insight on how to develop rational thinking for godly decision making. Philippians 4:8 says:

> Finally, brethren, whatever things are true, whatever things *are* noble, whatever things *are* just, whatever things *are* pure, whatever things *are* lovely,

whatever things *are* of good report, if *there is* any virtue and if *there is* anything praiseworthy—meditate on these things.

Think on these things only: whatever is true, honorable, fair, pure, acceptable, and commendable, if there is anything of excellence or anything praiseworthy. With great clarity and simplicity, we are told how to engage and develop our minds in rational thinking of the reasons for our actions. The more a person develops this habit, the better they become at making decisions that honor and please the Lord. Of course, habits are made through practice and repetition. There are many ways to grow this rational thinking habit, but I recommend beginning with the following simple steps. Take a blank piece of paper and make a list of up to three things that you know are not pleasing to God but you have found yourself doing multiple times in the past. This is not a list to condemn or judge you, but one to guide you to the right path. The Bible says that we (believers everywhere), have an Advocate with the Father—Jesus Christ the righteous, who is the propitiation (payment, appeasement, and atonement) for our sins (1 John 2:1–2).

Now, using Philippians 4:8 and other scriptures for each area of challenge, write down at least three reasons why you must *not* do this again. If there are reasons why these things may be good, write them down as well. Below is an example.

	Why it must stop	Why it's okay to continue
1. Watching porn	1. There is a sense of sin and guilt afterward. The Bible says anything done outside of faith is sin. (Romans 14:23)	1. Brings temporary relief
	2. It is impure. (Phil 4:8)	2. None
	3. I'm not proud of it. (Phil 4:8)	3. None

Continue with your list until you have fully thought through the challenges you want to address, and with the scriptures, outline the pros and cons for each.

At the very top of the list, write the text of 1 Corinthians 10:31 or use a similar text (this is my preference).

At the bottom of the page, write a scripture that affirms who you are in Christ. Second Corinthians 5:17 is one of my favorites.

"Therefore, whether you eat or drink, or whatever you do, do all to the glory of God." (1 Corinthians 10:31)

	Why it must stop	Why it's okay to continue
1. Watching porn	1. There is a sense of sin and guilt afterward. The Bible says anything done outside of faith is sin. (Romans 14:23)	Brings temporary relief
	2. It is impure. (Phil 4:8)	2. None
	3. I'm not proud of it. (Phil 4:8)	3. None
2. Spending a lot of time playing games and watching TV	1. It's a time waster.	It helps me to relax.
	2. I need to make a better use of my time. (Ephesians 5:16)	
	3. It's not on my list of priorities.	

"When someone becomes a Christian, he becomes a brand new person inside. He is not the same anymore. A new life has begun!" (2 Corinthians 5:17, TLB)

You have now developed your own rational thinking plan that is based on God's word and purpose for you. Now use this to challenge and pray for yourself as often as you can, reminding yourself that you are no longer subject to these things, but an overcomer through Christ Jesus.

Developing Persistence

The Lord Jesus presents for us a great model of perseverance and staying power. Hebrews 12:2 provides us with some insight into how He was able to persevere through a very difficult period of His earthly sojourn: "Looking unto Jesus, the author and finisher of *our* faith, who for the joy that was set before Him endured the cross, despising the shame, and has sat down at the right hand of the throne of God."

From this we can learn a few ways to develop similar traits of persistence and perseverance.

- Goal Setting

  It is pretty clear that our Lord and Savior came to the earth for a purpose. Everything He did was guided by that purpose. His responses and reactions were always in the context of how they fitted into His greater and singular purpose. Goal setting is as necessary to developing persistence and perseverance as fuel is to a car. Without clearly defined goals, there is nothing to work toward or sacrifice for. When the right goals are set, they determine the type of investments needed in order to achieve them. How do I set the right kinds of goals?

- Define your priorities

  What is important to you, and why? Are these things worth pursuing? How do these priorities measure against others? Your priorities describe who you are. They provide the reasons behind your decision making and create the pathway for your goals.

  It should be clearer now, I suppose, that the believer's first priority should be to please the Lord. But how does that translate to our day-to-day tasks and lives? Though there may be many ways I can please the Lord, the key question is what does He want me to do? What matters most to Him? Can I identify what these are specifically for me?

  Priorities can be very general or specific. For instance, a person might come to the conclusion that one of her important and foundational priorities is using her gifts to honor God. This is a great priority, but it is general in nature because it could have varied implications for the same person, depending on what the gifts or goals are. You can make the process of defining your priorities complicated and tenuous, or just take the less stressful but effective route of making a list. I call it simplified processing. What does this look like?

  - Make a list of your priorities. The order doesn't matter at this point. Keep it manageable. It should not exceed seven items.

- Now assign a number to the priorities in the order of their importance to you. How do you determine what is more important?
  - Identify core priorities. They are those that are foundational to the pursuit of other priorities. They may even be fundamental to who you are and what you believe. These should be assigned the lower numbers, typically from 1 to 3.
  - Stand-alone priorities should be assigned higher numbers like 6 or 7.
  - The lower the assigned number, the higher the priority should be.

My Priorities	Rating (1–7)
Please the Lord in all I do	1
Serve the Lord with my gifts, talents and abilities	4
Help others to know and experience the love of Christ	2
Be successful	6
Live a happy and fulfilled life	2
Live healthy	5

- Define your goals.
  Goals are task oriented. They are the specific objectives to be attained and clear milestones to be achieved.

Clearly defined goals are necessary for developing persistence and for progress. Your goals could be immediate, mid-term, or long-term. The longer the time required for its fulfillment, the higher the level of persistence required in order to succeed.

Consider the desired timing for the accomplishment of the identified goals. Rate each appropriately into one of the following categories:

- o Immediate (I): anything to be completed in less than a year
- o Mid-range (M): anything with a timeline of one to four years
- o Long-range (L): long-term priorities, typically spanning more than four years. These demand careful attention.

My Goals	Category (I/M/L)
Go to college and graduate with a good degree	M
Start a business in _____ after college	L
Share Christ with my friends	I
Improve on my skills/talents by practicing 30 minutes daily	I/M
Be deliberate in my decision making	I/M

- Assign the priorities to your goals.
  Match your goals to your priorities. The priority is the reason for pursuing the identified goal. When goals and priorities are properly matched, it provides the justification for committing to the actions needed to stay the course.

An understanding of the cost of the journey will enhance your ability to stay the course. There will be surprises along the way, but knowing and expecting these are vital to developing perseverance.

- Envision the end result.

  "Looking unto Jesus, the author and finisher of our faith, who for the joy that was set before Him endured the cross, despising the shame, and has sat down at the right hand of the throne of God" (Hebrews 12:2). Use your goals to create a vision of the end result. Jesus's vision included seeing many people from every nation on earth becoming children of God. That picture was so powerful that it enabled Him to endure a gruesome and unimaginably painful death.

  You can develop a similarly powerful picture, though the cost of attaining your vision may be far less than His. This is the work of faith. Faith creates a picture (substance) of a desired goal and enables you to enter into the future while it's yet far away. Developing the right goal and envisioning the end result with the eyes of the mind and spirit will give you enough material (evidence) to hold on to for as long as may be necessary. "Faith is the substance of things hoped for, the evidence of things not seen."

Your staying power is a direct result of the strength of your goals and the power of your vision. Set your goals properly by matching them with the right priorities, see clearly with the help of the Holy Spirit, and you will be able to endure the tests that seek to derail you on your life's journeys.

Avoiding Spiritual Myopia

> "For he who lacks these things is shortsighted, even to blindness, and has forgotten that he was cleansed from his old sins. Therefore, brethren, be even more diligent to make your call and election sure, for if you do these things you will never stumble; for so an entrance will be supplied to you abundantly into the everlasting kingdom of our Lord and Savior Jesus Christ." (2 Peter 1:9–11)

Who is a shortsighted Christian? It is the believer who is not growing in his or her relationship with God and is not making the right kind of investments into developing a godly character.

There are dangers to being shortsighted. One is that the person progressively gets worse without realizing it until a state of blindness is reached, where all sense of identity, value, and purpose is lost. This is a state of darkness and retrogression that every serious-minded person should do everything they can to avoid. There a few other implications and dangers to shortsightedness:

- Loss of the desire to please the Lord. Imperviousness to the promptings of the Holy Spirit.
- Loss of an appreciation for what truly matters in life.
- Indifference to sin—the person begins to find ways to justify, excuse, or explain it away.
- Loss of connection with God.
- Ultimately, falling back into the old ways sin and rebellion—forgets "that he was cleansed from his old sins."

We can we avoid these dangers by paying attention to making the right investments in our relationships with God, in our character, and in developing our relationships with others. We must place much value in knowing and doing these things, lest we forget who we are and lose out on God's blessings. Diligence and commitment to growth are required to overcome spiritual myopia.

"We become what we repeatedly do." (Sean Covey)

Chapter 6

INVESTING IN YOUR RELATIONSHIP WITH OTHERS

"Kindness is a language which the deaf can hear and
the blind can see." (Mark Twain)

THE FIRST ELEVEN VERSES OF 2 PETER CHAPTER ONE PROVIDE US
with two vital attributes that need to be developed in order to
grow positive and fruitful relationships with others. These attributes are kindness (or brotherly kindness) and Christian love.

Relationships are one of the unavoidable necessities of life. They
shape who we are and determine what we become. When a person
is invested in and surrounded with positive, enriching, and mutu-
ally beneficial relationships, his or her quality of life improves significantly. A group of researchers recently published their findings
supporting this in the *Social Science & Medicine Journal.*[1] Their findings are based on the analysis of Gallup data collected from 139
countries.

Life becomes richer, fuller, and more purposeful when we are invested in the right kinds of relationships. This is even more important for those of us who are believers in Christ. Our faith ushers us into what is a new, supremely vital, and continuously growing relationship with God and all His children. We are no longer alone, but part of a great family on earth and in heaven. The Apostle Paul captures this ever so clearly in his letter to the Ephesian church:

> Now you are no longer strangers to God and foreigners to heaven, but you are members of God's very own family, citizens of God's country, and you belong in God's household with every other Christian. (Ephesians 2:19, TLB)

What an awesome privilege it is! You are part of God's great family, regardless of where you were born, who your parents are, or what you might have done in the past. In Christ, you have a new identity and a new family fathered by the Almighty God himself. Awesome!

Being human, there are times when this family identity doesn't appear to be exciting or a welcome prospect. This is typically so when we come across people whose membership in this spiritual family we secretly doubt because of some character flaw, past mistakes, or some negative experiences we've had with them in the past. So how do we handle such situations? What can we do with such people?

Regardless of your perception or insight into their flaws, each one of us is challenged to first consciously and proactively invest in them through kindness and Christian love. I believe this is so because God is primarily interested in who you become and not necessarily what others may be doing, whether they are growing in their walk with Him or not. In other words, the Lord is focused on you—your walk with Him and your responsiveness to His desires for you. Romans 12:18 says, "As much as depends on you." You are God's focus. He's all about who you become and what you allow the Holy Spirit to do in you.

A Family Identity

Investing in others through kindness and love is the nature of God and His family. The Holy Spirit revealed the nature and character of God to us through His word. The Epistle of John stated that God is love, and anyone who does not practice love does not belong to Him (1 John 3:10 and 4:7–8). Love is the family identity. It identifies us to one another and to the world that we belong to God (John 13:34–34). Why, then, is this difficult to practice?

All our lives, we have been trained to be self-focused, self-seeking, and self-serving. These tendencies do not completely disappear because we are now born-again Christians. They are intrinsic to human nature and must be unlearned. Learning to be this new kind, generous, and loving person is a taxing but necessary process for every believer who desires to grow. A commitment to this process enables growth and begins with a new way of thinking.

Don't change yourselves to be like the people of this
world, but let God change you inside with a new
way of thinking. Then you will be able to understand and accept what God wants for you. You will
be able to know what is good and pleasing to him
and what is perfect. (Romans 12:2 ERV)

Change on the inside begins by filling my mind and thoughts
with God's word. As I have stated earlier, this begins by developing
the discipline of reading, meditating, and studying the Bible—
God's written word.

Developing Kindness

"Be kind, for everyone you meet is fighting a harder battle"
(Plato). Developing the attribute of kindness or brotherly affection
is a practical lifestyle-changing experience. It begins with adopting
a set of principles.

1. Treat others as you want to be treated.
    This is referred to as the Golden Rule. Jesus said it: "Do
    for others what you would want them to do for you. This
    is the meaning of the Law of Moses and the teaching of
    the prophets" (Matthew 7:12). Respect begets respect.
    Likewise, kindness begets kindness, and love begets love.
    The premise of this principle is that you desire to be treated
    with kindness and love. If that's the case, then you must first
    treat others the same.

2. Sow kindness, and you will reap what you sow.

Many times in our lives, sometimes even on a daily basis, we are provided with the opportunity to demonstrate kindness to others, including those who don't seem to deserve it. These opportunities are so easily ignored when we are not sensitive to the situation or feel there is no justification for it. No justification is needed for an act of kindness.

From simple acts like offering your seat in a crowded bus to a very consequential act like withholding judgment and condemnation, every act of kindness creates a ripple that will return to the giver in unexpected and immensely rewarding waves. Jesus' teaching in the sixth chapter of Luke, verses 36 through 38, emphasizes this principle.

Sow kindness by withholding judgment even when it is due. Sow kindness by showing mercy even when it is not deserved. Sow kindness through forgiveness. Sow kindness by lending a helping hand. Sow kindness by giving to others. It will make you a better Christian, and you will reap in the manner that you have sowed.

3. Be a good neighbor who is mindful of others.

    Jesus' parable of the Good Samaritan has earned an almost universal acceptance as a model for teaching compassion and care for others, no matter what they look like or where they come from. Christians typically wholly accept the teachings, but we tend to see it as applicable to us only in a limited sense, preferably when it does not cramp our lifestyles or encroach into our well-carved-out space.

Personally, I believe that the Lord is teaching me through His word and particularly through this parable that to show kindness:

- I need to slow down a bit and pay attention to others around me.
- I need to be sensitive to the pains and needs in the lives that I come across daily. He is not asking me to play God, but He is asking me to be human enough to listen to them and care for them within the limits of my ability.
- I need to first give my time, and then my energy, skill, and other resources as I am given the opportunity. Giving of one's time is one of the harder things to do.
- I need to make a personal commitment on the behalf of another. True kindness demands a personal commitment from me.
- I am my brother's keeper.

These are not easy to do. We struggle to bear our own burdens, and it is even more difficult to carry someone else's, but the Lord challenges us to bear none by ourselves (Matthew 10:28 and 1 Peter 5:7). He offers to carry all for us if we give them to Him. So as I lend a hand to assist someone, He (the Lord) is reaching out to that person through me, and I in turn must yield it all over to Him so that I don't collapse under a load He alone can carry easily.

Investing in Love

Many books have been written, and many messages have been preached on love. I believe that there is none better than the Bible at revealing the essence and the nature of God's kind of love—the kind He expects of every believer. John 3:16 and the thirteenth chapter of the First Epistle to the Corinthians, the two utmost love passages of the New Testament, reveal what love is and what it does and it doesn't do.

Do you see these qualities in yourself? Do you know how you can grow in these qualities of love? The Holy Spirit in the life of the believer is the guide, teacher, and nurturer of these traits. That's why we must rely on Him and live under His direction. As you follow Him on a daily basis, practice the steps outlined below. I call them the keys to investing in love.

1. Call forth these traits in yourself.

    This applies the principle of sowing in the kind you want to reap. The sowing in this instance is into your life by speaking and affirming to yourself the characteristics you want to see grow in yourself. How? Use "I" statements to personalize and affirm each trait you desire to grow in. Here are some I statements you can use:

"Love is patient. I have the love of God in me, so I am patient and continue to grow in patience."

"Love is kind. God's kindness is in me. I am kind, considerate, and loving."

"I have God's nature of love. I do not and cannot hate. I forgive (*you can say a name here*) completely, without reservation, because it is God's desire, and I choose to please Him." Continue with each specific trait and affirm repeatedly. Don't get tired or give up. By affirming these, you are training your mind to see and think differently. Affirm the nature of God in you, and you will become and reveal more of that which you affirm.

2. Be the first to act.

Don't wait. Christian love does not wait to be reciprocated or requited. It is always the first to act. "But God demonstrates His own love toward us, in that while we were still sinners, Christ died for us" (Romans 5:8). The Lord Jesus taught on this attitude (Luke 6:32–35), emphasizing that as God's children, we must be first to act in love, just as God our Father did. Be the first to forgive. Be the first to seek restoration. Be the first to seek peace. This is who your Father is, and it is how you must act.

Notes

1. Santosh Kumar et al., "Social support, volunteering and health around the world: Cross-national evidence from 139 countries," *Social Science & Medicine* Volume 74, Issue 5, (2012): 696–706, Accessed March 22, 2017, doi: 10.1016/j. socscimed.2011.11.017

BIBLIOGRAPHY

Wikipedia contributors, "Simone Biles," *Wikipedia, The Free Encyclopedia,* https://en.wikipedia.org/w/index.php?title=-Simone_Biles&oldid=782729183 (accessed March 22, 2017)

Anthony St. Peter, *The Greatest Quotations of All-Time* (Xlibris Corporation, 2010); 530

Santosh Kumar, Rocio Calvo, Mauricio Avendano, Kavita Sivaramakrishnan, and Lisa F. Berkman, "Social support, volunteering and health around the world: Cross-national evidence from 139 countries," *Social Science & Medicine* Volume 74, Issue 5, (2012): 696–706, Accessed March 22, 2017. doi: 10.1016/j.socscimed.2011.11.017

CPSIA information can be obtained
at www.ICGtesting.com
Printed in the USA
FSHW04n1021220318
46020FS